Free Verse Editions

Edited by Jon Thompson

Physis

Nicolas Pesquès

Translated and Introduced
by Cole Swensen

Parlor Press
West Lafayette, Indiana
www.parlorpress.com

Parlor Press LLC, West Lafayette, Indiana 47906

Printed in the United States of America
S A N: 2 5 4 - 8 8 7 9

Library of Congress Cataloging-in-Publication Data

Pesquès, Nicolas.
  [Face nord de Juliau, cinq. English. Selections]
  Physis / Nicolas Pesquès ; translated and introduced by Cole Swensen.
    p. cm. -- (Free verse editions)
  ISBN 978-1-932559-47-7 (pbk. : alk. paper) -- ISBN 978-1-932559-
48-4 (adobe ebook)
  I. Swensen, Cole, 1955- II. Title.
  PQ2676.E7829F3513 2007
  841'.914--dc22
                                        2007003543

Printed on acid-free paper.
Cover photograph by Nicolas Pesquès.
Book design by David Blakesley

Parlor Press, LLC is an independent publisher of scholarly and
trade titles in print and multimedia formats. This book is available in
print and Adobe eBook formats from Parlor Press on the Internet at
http://www.parlorpress.com. For submission information or to find out
about Parlor Press publications, write to Parlor Press, 816 Robinson St.,
West Lafayette, Indiana, 47906, or e-mail editor@parlorpress.com.

Contents

Introduction

This book is the fifth in an ongoing series titled *La face nord de Juliau*—Juliau is a mountain in the Ardèche in the south of France, and Pesquès' window looks out on its north face. He started writing this series about twenty-five years ago with the expressed intent of doing in words what Cézanne did with Mount St. Victoire in paint. What *was* Cézanne doing with that mountain? On the one hand, trying to grasp change. We all know that the world changes, yet somehow never get to see it doing so, but could that change be captured in the interstices of numerous images? Which brings us up against the question: is an image necessarily static? Or is there a way of rendering images that can capture their motion as well? We think of the motion picture, which we all know is composed of single images simply passing very quickly. Or so it was thought upon its invention toward the end of Cezanne's life.

In our own era, however, we have quite a different understanding, and different ways—digital and video—of capturing an image in its actual flow. But have we gotten any closer to capturing change, or even the object itself? Can the poetic image manage these feats that the visual image cannot?

Perhaps, but like Cézanne's work, Pesquès' also has a crisis of presence at its core, though it's a crisis that's meant to be enjoyed; it is crisis brought to a ringing pitch that translates to vividness, and this in itself increases the chances of presence. We are tricked, in lucky moments, into falling through the gaps—between brush-strokes, between words—into our own witnessing of the act of recording, and then this is the moun-

tain to which we have been brought—not the mountain that is
perceived, but that of perception itself.

Pesquès refers to this five-book series not as a project, but
as an adventure, which underscores two things—first, that an
end, a goal, is not part of the plan, and second, that there is no
plan. There is outward movement. And for Pesquès, moving
outward demands a collaboration with life, which he symbol-
izes by a partner object, suggesting that all exploration is based
on rapport. Like Cézanne, Pesquès found this partner object in
a mountain, a feature of the landscape that is both striking and
mundane—you see it everyday, and yet you're always stopped
by it, brought up short by it, and thus both subtly and suddenly
reminded of your own presence in the world, there facing this
mountain. Mountain: always irreducibly material and inescap-
ably metaphorical. A site of paradox, which, if it can be pre-
vented from falling into contradiction, is always fruitful.

Pesquès puts this paradox at the center of his adventure by
subtly working its metaphoric possibilities, paralleling the en-
counter with the mountain with an encounter with language,
for again like Cézanne, Pesquès realizes not only that any en-
counter with the world is mediated, but that that mediation is
as rich a mine of experience as is the ostensible object of at-
tention. Just as Cézanne lets us see the brush-strokes and the
dynamic relations of colors, Pesquès lets us see words in action;
his "word-strokes" are foregrounded throughout and keep us
conscious of the confines of language and of its constructive
role in the realities it describes.

And yet, we're also aware of the endlessness that language,
simultaneously, brings to things, of how, by multiplying points
of view, tones, approaches, by shifting from description to nar-
rative to analogy to reflection, it multiplies its subject. That
subject could be anything— mountain, moment, mouse—and
anything so thoroughly treated will reveal much about our re-
lationship to the world. The important thing is the constancy
of engagement. To look at a single thing under every light and
over much time is to demonstrate that no thing is ever single,

that, à la Heraclitus, even if you wanted to paint, write, see the same mountain twice, you could not.

This is the other thing that Cézanne was doing with his mountain—exploring the effect of sheer multiplicity, intimately documenting the trajectory of a repetition, capturing that other paradox, the simultaneous cyclical and linear shape of a series. But is seriality in poetry possible in the way that it is in painting? To get beyond this apparent impossibility is to bring a different kind of time to poetry, to insist on a temporal compression equal to the temporal extension that poetry can't get away from. And it is to refuse exhaustion, to say that we can never get to the end of even the simplest object, which is then in turn always a celebration, not only of that object, but by extension, of all the elements of the world.

And it is to that actual world, the *physis* of the ancient Greek system, that Pesquès always turns our attention. In this book, that world is dominated by the vivid yellow of the Scotch broom that blooms all over the hillside in late spring; other books in the series are dominated by green. In all, color functions as another limit, parallel to the limits of language, but a little more visible, and older, even older than the limits of experience. Color is the first of the visual stimuli registered by the brain—even before movement, long before line, color presents itself, and so it readily becomes the rich medium of a relentless affection, first Pesquès', but soon, too, our own, as our attention becomes, in turn, part of his world, and our reading becomes part of the poem. For what starts as description fails as it turns into life, as it becomes not a description of something else, but a vital thing-in-the-world in its own right. Which leaves us, though with a poem, without the mountain. And so Pesquès' exploration goes on, reaching through book after book toward a single thing, and gathering instead all that that thing becomes in order to avoid capture.

Physis

One

From the hill, only the veined wording
the atmospheric seed
and the stones begin again

. . .

the stones would be painted; you could breathe them in

by frightened abstraction
by solitude

. . .

the sentences watch where I fall

each time the torch flares up

the eyes times five
give and give
in spite of the hill
the imperceptible, the separable

. . .

one by one, upending their dependence

grass, clouds, woods

. . .

to each his own eye
will touch the untried color
will dismember deepest night

the illegibility of the cut and the thirst
at each syllable
one by one
of the hammered pleasure

of a single saturated yellow

. . .

sex of the path that turns

that rises to the quake

sex of the story from inside the story

the verb, carried to the close
gnaws at death
geometrizes flesh

. . .

sentences, sentences
like dirt tossed out of a grave
the futurgenic dirt

like a cloud is seeded
the black juice of grammar
corners ardor in a face

physis

as are thoughts

goddesses

nonsuited, distended

identities forgotten in their blood

their ghosts lying in the meadow
in its curves

. . .

no longer only face to face
with the insistent and silent hill

but an extension
infinitely visible

the reading of a chlorophyllic era

physis

as are commas, loves, the logic of stones

here and there the same sparkling wall
the same pleasures aborted in the light

the same dissection of repetition and joy

. . .

like a membrane between language and shadow
who severs life, distributes beauty

measured by neither the sentence nor the hill

. . .

a pin stuck in your neck, a stake for the goat
in a circle stunned by childhood
peddling forgetting
tattooing forgetting

language among all physis
as much colored grass
as wizard at the foot of the wall

caught between sky and earth
tightened to the breath
of a cut bouquet

. . .

the interstice, abyss of fresh earth
dilating, constricting
keeping
all the promises of impossibility

the ravaged liaison, the radical fusional strangeness
leaving unguided lightning
between us

such a snake slicing
through the glade of rift

and the rigid ruins of pride

one by one   boned   blind
that the sentence will have no more to separate
but can mine from the ravine
and plunge again into the fear
of marrying no more

therefore
I need five times unstable dependence
diplomacy so extreme
it can precede forgetting
lift all holds on expression

find idioms, greens, loves
that can withstand the scene

. . .

such a play of junctions
such a realm of torment

thought   on its knees   calm
its insides churning
schematizing blue, the sheets,
the crime

. . .

only at the order of a glance
each thing admitting no more than one word at a time
than a single ultimate pink

precipice, one by one propelling

body fallen into resonance, dismantled diction
cheeks on fire, breasts cherry
blindly recording the face of vertigo

Two

To write, train only with the intense
whose power is color, whose color is an order

such an easy obscurity amid what the body does:
the syntax of reflex
the uncommonly talented yes

a procession
in the heart each time dark
in the exaggerated dark that replaces writing

. . .

unfurls, with the hill, a sovereign yellow

its explosion alone where the eyes follow

to say it's just like that outside is never certain
outside includes, is an invented yellow that could go first

one by one cannot be revived

only the frames of love exist
and claim resemblance

and unleash these claims

could it be that it's someone else who watches
writes, veers?
some in rags who attack me
scattering shame and crushing

. . .

with local burning
with an intimacy that will owe its subtlety to grammar

this hill is also yours
exuberant
in each whole world

a sentence is a landscape, as is a color
they can become the sky
they can regain the child

they're enough to cause

that stone sound they make between them
one by one
with a sudden surge of ground water
is a billion mothers
in the wreck of a single image

physis

as are the unities

the destruction of the center

the sentimental things

what I say of color is muscle,
without caring if it's really a hill
or even what a hill is

we must isolate the painful part of passing into words
and if we can build upon this passage

if language errs in regretting the separation
and does it violence in desiring it erased
while the world is equal
plus the pain of that equation, plus the way that pain is made

sometimes I use words like cubes
sometimes like they're rag pickers

suckling, beneath the belly of grammar,
the monogamous night where they keep on drowning

sinking in and tossing out

ending plays no part. dying just sets them off

to make frequent grammatical errors
is to come too fast and too often

there are insensible stretches that come long before the statement
and that follow even longer
they're the entourage in the middle of which
someone sometimes points to the color of pain
the violence of yellow

the same thing as the field's force
when the verb circles like a vulture
and I enter the voluptuous air

. . .

yellow has scattered its lightning languor

there's another way to say it, a way inflammable and fixed
which is to have it silently consumed while it seems to be ascending

just as in nature
with its moments that make you, suddenly, want to write it

suddenly is everything that the statement sinks into

be it a wall
be it a dissolve into light air

here and there the body flies into disbelief. and has no fear.

why do I bow before this green, why does yellow tremble in me?
and how can I get over it
and why do I feel better not knowing

. . .

but we no longer want to hover
between flare and flare
nor to keep on dreading the light

a lack of fear is more dangerous still
with its gaping phrase
gaining unreasonable speed
toward a landscape

with three concomitant things:
grammatical terror
suspicion of other worlds
and the conventional task of naming all this

from a certain angle all color is mass

in the photo the phrases are what they are
the words can't manage to do anything but

exhausting images, yellow in suspension
towed along by an articulation

drifts out of sight
one by one
toward the ink roller

the body fitter, the factory of earth

*"I want to grasp the things of the spirit just as
the vagina grasps the penis"*

not images but impressions,
engravings, flow

one by one
no longer resisting
through a narrative facade
or fabrication

with expressions re-natured
a kind of diagrammatic yellow
carving reservoirs on loved surfaces

the cruel abundance
of the tall slick Scotch broom where I pass
from numbness to writing
to the missing glance

deep cliff, smile that pours forth

aligning its angles

. . .

the softness of this surround
right next to the eye in flight in opening the sky

this block of language on its mute gate

the optics of the word includes no cone
but a color
stamping dryly, accelerating depth

and a grass snake of breath
until the hill stops replying to the call of the eye

but renews
denudes the venom

from yellow to the same yellow

what has disappeared holds up the exhausted body

a spray of yellow among bifurcations

on tip-toe, right next to the lie,
behind a single shoulder, grazed against
something not quite heard

in contemplation, nature passes on the other side.
at the same time, the rip gets louder.
it becomes the bone of phrase and earth. it tends the mourning heat,
the depth of the tie, the corner of the spoken.
it makes landscape into grief's *traveling,* and matter ignites.

a love facing
eyes in the lost
raised by what separates

. . .

the one of whom
this diver, this drowned

the one between the legs of which
Venusian, vile, Venusian, vile
burned rose, white cheeks

watching it oscillate

to write: to get lost with extreme precision

to write to the red light
thereby emptying the view

. . .

push the color toward the hands
make the sentence cross the stage

so that at the end, something you can't see looks like

. . .

at the end, they have eyes for it. overruns the body.
yellow coats the angles. you see like you read.

the joy of broom staples two memories together
one unable to remember the other.

I fight to bring the places back

so that yellow means not only broom
but a sting, a move made tangible

that's what's stifling, what's clinging,

yet, I'd like to keep the depth of field
beyond the eyes the same
with the amplitude of *swing* and all the armory of hips

. . .

with color, water starts to run again;
the ammonite spreads. I return to the escape.

as if it were a matter of witnessing the arrival of a phrase
to muzzle a force before its design.

Three

Two empires tangled: outside, the one of images
that faces, fertilizes, and frisks the other

a single body entangled
that wants to graft, to surpass
that wants to open its legs

language that swoops down on the yearnings of earth

. . .

all leap forward: the fire of eyes, the forehead and the fracture
in the image plane there's the blazing bolt
the depth of stone

memory waters only a single instant
landscape doesn't last
the hill is a centrifuge of short sentences
whose color comes back full circle
insistent as pain

at the heart of the solenoid
writing produces only blockades of light
the rain of sparks has no way out

first I ate the Scotch broom's wood
and then the poem that goes with it
the times are curiously similar

to go with, to fold up the sounds,
the statues' dresses
to adorn the devouring eye with shadows

all that crossed by color
along a chain of distribution
that returns to the same, to the surface of books,
changing its nature

because, one by one, the senses open their eyes
we can't help viewing the words
with a suspicion shot through with witness

they are neons, psychic congestion
swig taken backwards
beyond, writing will be metallic and robotic

. . .

permanent threats: unable to restore the suckling
forced to disconnect from the carpet of flesh
nailed by rapture

I write in lemon juice and sable

describe the wood of the Scotch broom
as something formless

I say yellow precisely for that reason
I touch the tender internal resistance

to write beyond is an architecture
to see nothing but to see
a sort of edgeless chessboard
labyrinthine

. . .

the yellow laquer at the end
such a decoration

that makes the hill into a glacial objective

a face and an arrhythmia
the reversible extension of a curve toward pink

to want at all cost to touch the scent, to smell the words, etc.
to love to see them doing it and even more
like *long ago*

protozoan plunged into color

I walk through the yellow beating it back, I write it askew
jungle is monochrome

I can't put the word before the hold
nor the hold before the memory's turmoil
and the panic of the glance that breaks up there

there's a sensibility that the senses can't attain
it invents itself in the expression

there's a cistern in the middle of the sentence
a metal in the field
it's all that the body's grace can't understand

the scattered landscape, embodied in pieces

block yellow, never familiar caress

. . .

I watch the electrolysis of color

as it vitrifies the phrases

it's possible to feel a blue
above summer
in a way distinctly polar

to feel it going numb

faced with a landscape that never settles
the words are decisive

it's a matter of constantly erasing thirst
by graphic pumping and accentuation

here, an infinitive: to write
and yet two more: to see, to close the eyes
a kind of gaze that could move a hill

by working the very matter of this yellow
on the table
I hold back the homonyms

. . .

"fixing with the gaze the very thing the word names"

at every moment the spark
a fire, a claim, a desire for yellow

a yellow to drink, a broom to come

. . .

to not see what they fix
but what happens with and around
that dissipates with them

yellow is the first to explode
because it's removed

by machine and by flame

now I know that I look inside
with eyes that have stopped wanting

pink brown of the previous scene
sundrenched pot where the hill begins

always a *print preview*

the senses have eyes for that
columns of love, territories of sparrow hawk

the sentences follow
they crush the starring of the senses' witnesses
they enlarge the fractures
the color spreads through their limbs

the tenacity of yellow
the people of the meadow

so much resistance and so much and
so much and that ignites

forgetting trembles, the yellow breath

sight would like to turn away from memory's injustice

but an instant won't get it there
if not shuddering from everywhere
reading the fever in a branch of broom

physis

as are the gusts, the functions,
the raspberries

embodied is the phrase that escapes to the flux
extending it by a strike

such the arrest and its satisfaction
a slow leap over interruption
a crossing of real yellow

its scintillating thirst, its married shade

are they not but the eyes' hopes
an open grave at each alliance
at each colorful spray?

. . .

the incline of this force has no skeleton

the more tempting, the more in error:
to separate the water from its muscle of earth
and then from its sentence

eye poker
for passing to the shadow of sensations
as if they were well-springs

the schism of love
under the argumentative hand
each eye enchanted by the drop to drop

. . .

as I cross the yellow
I do two things at once:
love and landscape

and so night arrives at the threshold of memory
unable to become a memory

it encroaches

"a sweet meadow between the gilded ice and the pure sky"

happiness compressed

and see how all the consequences of yellow are springs
how pain, with great finesse, turns blue

. . .

chewing and speaking have the same ending
they produce the ungraspable
whether we eat it
or it rejects us

each time that we open our mouths
we provoke a new world

only the shadows embrace

what yellow bears is lit up by the wrenching split

a skinless body

physis is the conjunction

physis is the third term
once the broom dissolves
once the love and once the landscape

the following is founded on the hardness of words

this clearing is the most uncontrollable

this forest floor that dilutes
this shadow yellow that builds up

toward the written
is elevation without religion

. . .

and thus the shock of the like:
this world here with its tools: eyes, sentences
the same yellow once they're arranged

now the wood hides the axiom

mountain with no particular essence
body reduced to expansion
to the leveling sovereignty of dust

on which language lines up imperatives:
textually they're husks
visually a cleaning

to question again without insistence
without turning the verbal form against itself
nor silencing
nor to write hauling it all along

. . .

ambient violence that wants to impose the hill upon me
monstrous yellow that wants to weaken me
break my coherence
that wants to pull me together by injecting me with a dismembering force

inaccessible body that asks nothing but existence
that throws desire to the colors
as if visibility could resolve presence

color is memory, that which retains only what exists
before memories

it precedes the landscape; it anticipates its divisions
color is already an image

then this is a forest, a field, a Scotch broom

. . .

it is also the last image. the easiest death.
the welcome to afterward. the eternal bed.

In life, it is the incalculable progeny.
it is precision and millions

pointed yellow that draws blood
yellow out loud

the hill's frequency, its deceptions
and its summits, is in the eyes

and it's not just the eyes that make this possible
but all visibility

yellow like a forecast of broom
green like an always future hill

Biographical Note

Nicolas Pesquès was born in France in 1946, and has been publishing poetry since 1971. His most recent books include *Trois poèmes (Three Poems)* from Edition du Limon, 1995, and *La face nord de Juliau un, deux, trois,* and *quatre* (*The North Face of Juliau One, Two, Three,* and *Four*), all published by André Dimanche Editeur in 1988, 1997, and 2000. *La face nord de Juliau cinq,* from which this text is taken, is due out later this year from the same publisher. Pesquès also writes literary and art criticism, and has published books on the work of visual artists Gilles Aillaud, Anne Deguelle, Jan Voss, and Aurélie Nemours, and on the poet Jacques Dupin. He divides his time between Paris and the Ardèche.

CPSIA information can be obtained at www.ICGtesting.com
Printed in the USA
LVOW07s0251200114

370117LV00002B/121/A

9 781932 559477